New Harbinger Journals for Change

Research shows that journaling has a universally positive effect on mental health. But in the midst of life's difficulties—such as stress, anxiety, depression, relationship problems, parenting challenges, or even obsessive or negative thoughts—where do you begin? New Harbinger *Journals for Change* combine evidence-based psychology with proven-effective guided journaling techniques to help you make lasting personal change—one page at a time. Written by renowned mental health and wellness experts, *Journals for Change* provide a creative and safe space to process difficult emotions, work through challenges, reflect on what matters, and set intentions for the future.

Since 1973, New Harbinger has published practical, user-friendly self-help books and workbooks to help readers make positive change. Our *Journals for Change* offer the same powerfully effective tools—without ever *feeling* like therapy. If you're committed to improving your mental health, these easy-to-use guided journals can help you take small, actionable steps toward lasting well-being.

For a complete list of journals in our *Journals for Change* series, visit newharbinger.com.

"Brilliant, compassionate, and challenging in all the right ways! The thought-provoking prompts and guided exercises provide a safe space for readers to explore the then-and-now impact of being raised by emotionally immature parents. The audacious challenges and objective reflections bring healing and growth in a wonderfully refreshing way. This guided journal isn't just about healing; it's about helping us reclaim our narrative and rediscover the resilient spirit within us!"

> —**Nicole Johnson, LPC, MEd, CCTP, CLC**, "The Ginger Shrink," and owner of Oak and Ivy Therapy Services

"Often when surrounded by emotionally immature people, we take on their criticism and commentary as our inner critic. The work in this book shows you how to inoculate yourself to the noise of the emotionally immature person, build your immunity to their efforts to control and overpower you, and recruit your inner critic to be your biggest fan while building trust in yourself and your intuition."

> —**Meagen Gibson**, chief content officer at Conscious Life, and cohost of Trauma Super Conference

"Gibson's journal is the missing link to achieve emotional healing from being raised by an emotionally immature parent. This guided journal gives readers the opportunity for deep self-reflection and understanding. Each chapter has thought-provoking questions, exercises, and education as to how children of emotionally immature parents can connect to their inner guidance and repair damage that was caused by their parents. Healing is possible with this remarkable companion journal."

> —**Brie Turns-Coe, PhD, LMFT**, chair of the marriage and family therapy program at Arizona Christian University; and author of *Parent the Child You Have, Not the Child You Were*

"As a psychologist, I enthusiastically recommend this guided journal for any clients who seek a deeper understanding of their complicated relationship with their emotionally immature parents. As a writer, I'm in awe of the skill and creativity Gibson employs to encourage thoughtful introspection while sharing transformative guidance. And as the target audience for this topic, I plan to revisit this journal time and time again."

—**Ryan Howes, PhD, ABPP**, clinical psychologist, and author of *Mental Health Journal for Men*

"More like life-changing therapy than a self-care book. Lindsay Gibson has created a safe, nurturing, therapeutic space for us to acknowledge our inner experiences, explore how our early relationships shaped us, and discover our truest selves deep within. Empowering, challenging, and healing, I found myself vitalized yet also unexpectedly grounded and humbled. Prepare yourself for a transformational experience!"

—**Holly Spotts, PsyD**, clinical psychologist, and owner of Full Cup Wellness

"Lindsay Gibson's *Adult Children of Emotionally Immature Parents Guided Journal* is an essential resource for anyone in the process of healing from neglectful parenting. As a therapist, I use Gibson's methods for clients who struggle to feel love and belonging in their broken family systems. Gibson's journal is filled with her trademark wisdom, wit, and kindness, and is a beautiful companion piece to her extensive work on adult children of emotionally immature parents."

—**Erin McMenamin, MSW**, licensed clinical social worker specializing in the treatment of post-traumatic stress disorder (PTSD) in the veteran population; and coauthor of *Entering the Parlor*

Adult Children *of* Emotionally Immature Parents

GUIDED JOURNAL

*Your Space
to Heal, Reflect
& Reconnect with
Your True Self*

LINDSAY C. GIBSON, PsyD

New Harbinger Publications, Inc.

Publisher's & Author's Note

This publication is designed to provide accurate and authoritative information in regard to the subject matter covered. It is sold with the understanding that the publisher and author are not engaged in rendering psychological, financial, legal, or other professional services. This guided journal is not intended to be psychotherapy or a substitute for psychotherapy. If expert assistance or counseling is needed, the services of a competent professional should be sought.

NEW HARBINGER PUBLICATIONS is a registered trademark of New Harbinger Publications, Inc.

New Harbinger Publications is an employee-owned company.

Cover design by Sara Christian

Interior design by Amy Shoup

Acquired by Tesilya Hanauer

Edited by Karen Schader

Printed in the United Kingdom

26   25   24

10   9   8   7   6   5   4   3   2

*Thank you, dear reader, for bringing
your heart and soul to this work.*

*May it support you in reclaiming a life
that will truly be your own.*

Contents

How You Are Impacted by Emotionally Immature Parents and How You Can Mature Past Their Influence

Using this journal, you're about to become a self-made person through introspection, reflection, and writing. This is your time to reconnect with your inner truth and to create a self-concept that finally reflects you accurately. Once you start to think about and question what you've been told about life, love, and yourself, your answers will spark a personal renaissance. In this journal, we're going to explore how you were impacted by emotionally immature (EI) parents and how you can mature past their influences.

· ·

A journal is for waking yourself up to who you really are.

· ·

Why Journaling Is Especially Helpful to Adult Children of Emotionally Immature Parents

The point of such inner exploration is lost on emotionally immature people (EIPs). They're not looking for self-discovery; they crave certainty and they insist on being right. They rarely self-reflect because that might introduce new ideas and uncertainty—an unsettling and unwanted prospect. Since EIPs are not psychologically growth-minded or introspective about their own lives, they repeat and relive the same narrative over and over again—and they expect you to go along with it. Their view of themselves and others never deepens; it just maintains its stereotyped, one-dimensional superficiality.

EIPs are skeptical of—even hostile to—the inner psychological world of other people (Gibson 2015; Shaw 2014). They dislike thinking about anything that isn't directly relevant to them. In contrast, if you are an internalizer type of adult child of emotionally immature parents (ACEIPs), you *are* deeply aware of what goes on inside you, enabling you to use self-reflection to understand yourself. With journaling, you can expand your self-awareness, learn from your experiences, validate your perceptions, reverse the impact of EIPs on your life, and take conscious control over your life choices.

The simple act of putting pen to paper affirms the worth of your thoughts and feelings. When you journal about your inner experiences—your thoughts, feelings, and wishes—you connect with yourself and realize that you have a right to be here, a right to your feelings, and a right to consider your life as important as anyone else's. Getting your experiences down on paper gives you perspective and a chance to feel deeper empathy for yourself.

> *Journaling is your decision to honor your inner life.*

Journaling is not a superficial pursuit, a little make-work activity to while away the time. It is an encounter with your soul—or whatever you call your spark of absolute individuality—in all its known and unknown aspects. Journaling offsets the invalidation of EIPs who predictably scoff at any time spent on self-exploration. They think they're doing fine without thinking about their inner psychological world, even as other people pay the price of their unawareness. But you know better. If you're an internalizer, you know from experience that your inner life is the wellspring of your happiness and self-actualization, not to mention your ability to love others. By writing in this journal, you are honoring the crucial importance of your inner life.

Your Never-Ending Development as a Person

As a child you sought your parents' approval because every child's development is fueled by their parents' love and admiration. Even if the relationship is not very nurturing, the child of EI parents will create a *healing fantasy* to make up for it (Gibson 2015). They hope that the parent will one day change and be able to give them that nurturing connection and support. The false promise of healing fantasies is that one day you will find a way to engage their attention and finally get close to them.

But your emotional maturity as an adult is *not* dependent on your EI parent's recognizing your worth and giving you permission to grow. You can grow and develop yourself right now without their help. You don't need an EIP's permission for that. In fact, you can do it over their explicit objections.

Each one of us has a unique psychological maturational drive orchestrated by something within us that pushes us to know ourselves, master reality, and handle adult problems and responsibilities (Anderson 1995). This inner push comes from what I call the higher or true self, but you may have other names for whatever it is in you that seeks expansion, competence, and meaningful living. This journal is designed to assist you in developing your individuality and lifelong psychological maturation—enabling you to grow into an emotionally mature person.

Maturity is not some stuffy endpoint in life where we dig in and start rigid-ifying into old patterns. On the contrary, it's the never-ending unfolding of self-discovery, creativity, and competence in living. Growing up with EIPs can convince you that maturation is a dull affair, a dead-end street where playfulness and pleasure gradually roll to a stop. In fact, one of the most critical things an EIP can think to say to you is, "You've changed."

Growing up is not only for the young, but for every adult who wants to mature into a fuller human being.

But true *maturation* is not the same as *encultura-tion*, that inexorable social process by which you are trimmed to fit the mold. Self-discovery is an exciting, vitalizing process, no matter what you find, because it's inherently energizing and strengthening to learn more about yourself and the world you live in. True maturation wakes you up to your individuality, enriches your mind, and seeks out the world's opportunities.

Outlet vs. Growth Journaling

A journal as an *outlet* can be tremendously helpful for expressing yourself safely and clarifying your thinking when you're in the middle of tumult or have to make a big decision. In this book, I plan to show you another kind of journaling that can actually change your life—guided *growth* journaling. Growth journaling can help you tap into the intuitive guidance of your higher self. We all have this inner growth drive to develop psychologically, but EIPs keep ignoring it while others, like you, pursue it to become more of who you were meant to be.

Your biggest psychological task in life is to discover your true self—that firm sense of who you really are. Nothing really goes right without it. I hope to create with you in this journal a structured path forward with a specific goal in mind: to actualize and empower your sense of self in the deepest possible way. To do that, you must

Anytime you honestly answer the right question, you change yourself.

understand and reverse the impact of the EIPs in your life. These journaling prompts will speed your development by encouraging you to find the right words for your experiences—words to make you feel understood by yourself.

This journal will help you discover a healthy, sturdy sense of self that is immune to the control of EIPs. The journal's purpose is to support you in being there for yourself. It will chronicle your journey all in one place, holding a record of your thoughts, and serving as a reference point as you chart your course. You're about to write your way into an empowered connection with who you truly are and what you want to become.

How to Use This Journal

As you engage with the questions and prompts, imagine that you're telling someone—me, a friend, your higher self—what you're feeling. This will make your journal entries more immediate, intimate, and down-to-earth. Keep it simple and heartfelt; don't let your wordy brain go off on abstract essays. The goal is not to write *about* something, but to try to write *from* your heart. We're not speculating on ideas here; we're trying to get closer to the emotional truth. Generalities about yourself won't help you as much as getting at the specifics of your life *experiences*. Keep it direct and real. If you write honestly from your feelings, you'll build a solid platform of self-awareness from which you can continue your growth. Your unique inner world will feel invigorated, and you'll feel increasingly psychologically real to yourself (Shaw 2014).

In addition to self-discovery in each journal section, you'll have opportunities to practice new modes of thought and to reclaim positive feelings of empowerment and self-affection. Each part begins with memories about how you've been affected and then explores new outlooks and solutions. By practicing new thought patterns and speaking them out loud, you will dislodge old mental habits and develop constructive attitudes for the future. By reflecting on and copying down new concepts, you will start to own new ideas about yourself through the physical act of writing, as the motion of your hand commits real intention to those thoughts.

Throughout the journal, we'll also imagine how your parents might respond if asked how they thought of you or how they tried to help you mature. This perspective will give you a feel for how they considered—or didn't—your inner experiences and their important role in supporting your future self-concept. In addition, we'll envision some third-party observations of you as a child so that you can feel real empathy for the predicaments of your childhood.

Interestingly, however, you may find that just *reading* some journal prompts will trigger change in you. Don't feel you have to write out each and every answer in order. Write when it helps you to think it out. You might feel the urge to go back later and fill in the ones you left blank, and that's fine too.

You may even find that you have more to record about your self-discoveries than this journal has space for. Don't waste these discoveries! Be prepared with another notebook or affix large sticky notes in the journal on which you can record additional thoughts. You can also visit http://www.newharbinger.com /53004 to download and print copies of the empowerment statements and more space to practice speaking back to the EIP in your life or the EIP voice in your head.

Get ready to explore the impact EIPs have had on your life, how you grew up to think of yourself, and who you want to become in the future. You may even discover that your past has accelerated your maturity and self-sufficiency in important ways, in spite of the difficulties. Who knows? Your EI parents may have unwittingly bequeathed you superpowers, not just problems. You never know what unexpected gifts might come from the hardship of dealing with such parents.

We're about to reverse all that has sent you into hiding. Are you ready to go find yourself? **Let's get started.**

PART I

Know Yourself and Don't Let Go of Who You Are

EI parents treat children in such superficial, coercive, and judgmental ways that they undermine their children's ability to trust their own thoughts and feelings, thereby restricting the development of their children's intuition, self-guidance, efficacy, and autonomy.

—Recovering from Emotionally Immature Parents (p. 2)

You learn who you are from the people closest to you. While growing up, with every look and action toward your parent, you were asking them: *Who am I? React to me so I can know myself.* If your parents were emotionally immature, they had a hard time making you feel seen as a real individual. Beyond superficial praise or punishment, they lacked the awareness that they also had a duty to help you build a positive self-concept, mature reality awareness, and a capacity to enjoy life with zest. Without adequate adult feedback about your qualities and who you were becoming, you might have grown up with a distorted or incomplete sense of your true self. And without that strong sense of self, it's hard to fully feel both your value and your vitality.

EI parents are always ready to tell you what to do, who you should be, and what you should want. But this constant influencing makes it hard for you to know yourself because their opinions become internalized as a kind of automatic mental voice. With all this judgmental input during childhood, you hesitate to trust your own sense of self. When the EIP voice in your head starts talking, it can be very hard to hear yourself over it. Fortunately, your journaling here will amplify your own thoughts so that you can feel more confident about what you really believe.

Knowing yourself—having an accurate, informed self-concept—is crucial for your relationships too. Your self-awareness gives you power to not only develop yourself but also to be aware of your effect on others and how they are feeling. To imagine others' feelings, you have to be in touch with your own. Self-knowledge is therefore not a frivolous bonus feature, but an essential element in your ability to form your deepest human connections.

Now let's look at how EI parents may have impacted your ability to know yourself and your own potential. Later we'll also look at how they may have affected your self-confidence and sense of belonging.

Don't overthink the next two questions: it works best to write down what comes to mind *first*.

If I interviewed your mother when you were growing up, how might she have completed the following description of you?

My child is _____

_____

_____

_____

If I asked your father for a description of you, what might he have said about you?

My child is _____

_____

_____

_____

Looking back, what did your parents not realize about you? Complete this thought:

They had no idea that I was so _____

_____

_____

_____

What were some of the nonverbal ways your parents communicated how they saw you? (For example, rolling their eyes when you offered an opinion, frowning when you asked questions.)

_____

_____

_____

Off the top of your head, come up with a thought to complete each of the following:

To my mother, it was like I was a _____ .

To my father, it was like I was a _____ .

In which of the following ways did your parents affect you? Check all that apply.

☐ They actively diminished or wounded my image of myself.

☐ They neglected helping me know myself at all.

☐ They gave me distorted feedback about who I was that didn't fit me.

Pretend you're a fly on the wall observing yourself as a child in your family. What was it like for that little kid growing up around people who didn't get them or show interest in their thoughts and feelings? Write your observations in the third person ("she was"/"he was"/"they were"), describing what it would have been like for that child growing up in that atmosphere.

_____

_____

_____

....

_____

....

_____

What have you done as an adult that might come as a surprise to your parents,
based on what they expected of you?

_____

....

_____

....

_____

What was your most important potential that they overlooked?

_____

....

_____

....

_____

Now think about an important teacher or mentor in your life, someone who did see and support your potential. If I interviewed them, what might *they* tell me about you?

With or without your parents' help, you've been accumulating self-knowledge and self-awareness all your life. You need *self-awareness* to sense your feelings and true reactions. You need *self-knowledge* (truths you know about yourself) to construct your self-concept—your sense of who you are and what you can do. Tell me about the qualities in yourself that you're proud of, as well as the areas in which you want to improve.

I'm proud of

I want to become more _____

_____

_____

_____

_____

_____

_____

_____

_____

· · · · · · · · · ·

*By getting to know
yourself better, I
wonder what qualities
you will add to your
self-concept today.*

· · · · · · · · · ·

Do you think your current self-concept reflects who you really are, or does it reflect old self-images influenced by an EIP's attitude toward you?

_____

_____

_____

_____

_____

_____

Write a brief rough draft about who you are as a person, your self-concept. You are a work in progress, but just say what you know about yourself so far; for example, "I take other people's feelings into account and I enjoy meaning-ful conversations." I'll get you started with some fill-ins below, and then you can go on from there:

I am the kind of person who enjoys _____

but I've never been very interested in _____ .

I would love it if everyone would stop expecting me to _____

_____

_____

_____

_____

_____

I pretty much live my life by these values: _____

_____

_____

_____

_____

_____

Think back over the past few days. Find three situations that revealed your good character—your best qualities as a person—as you went about your life. Jot down the good qualities you noticed in yourself, as well as other memories that illustrated these qualities. Later in part 9, when we explore how you treat yourself when you make mistakes, you'll have the chance to describe other, more self-critical thoughts. But for now, journal about the good things you realized about yourself looking back.

I'm happy to realize about myself that I

Read the following empowering statement, and if you agree, say it out loud and copy it down with intention to claim it as a guiding belief for the future: *I am entitled to listen to my own instincts and to be my true self with other people. There is nothing inherently selfish about knowing who I am and what I want.*

We can internalize EIPs' attitudes without even noticing it. Their statements can turn into an inner voice that undermines our confidence. As you do these writing prompts, is there a mocking, self-defeating voice in your head that is making fun of this quest to know your true self? If you hear that voice inside your mind, perhaps it's making remarks like: *What a waste of time! You know all you need to know about yourself. Stop writing in that book and do something productive!*

Nobody gets to tell you self-knowledge is unimportant.

If so, here's your chance to stand up for yourself in your own mind. Forcefully talk back to this derogatory mental voice that undermines your efforts at building self-awareness. (Put some heat on it: your actual authority figure will never read this.)

Write down three discouraging things that the self-defeating voice in your head tells you about your interest in self-knowledge:

1. _____

2. _____

3. _____

Now for each one, refute it and counter it with a more accurate statement.

1. _____

2. _____

3. _____

You can't let those head voices run your life. Speak up and ask some impertinent questions to those internalized EI authority figures in your head who have continued to control you by discouraging you from building your self-knowledge:

Hey, what gives you the right to _____?

Wait, who says I can't _____?

How come you get to _____ *and I'm not allowed to*

_____?

• •

EI people often judge other people's rights and opinions as a form of impertinence against them.

• •

Not only can you challenge their disrespect of your self-discovery, you can strengthen your sense of self with assertive thoughts. Make the claim that your personhood is worthy of being known. Stand up for your right to understand yourself:

From now on, you don't get to _____ .

It's my duty to get to know myself so I can _____ .

You can't make me _____ .

Tell me truthfully why *you* think having a closer relationship with yourself and getting to know yourself better would be good for you. Think about it for a minute, then do your best to convince me.

_____

_____

_____

_____

> *You can reset your self-concept anytime you want, no matter who has invalidated or minimized who you are.*

_____

What feelings has this subject stirred up in you so far?

_____

_____

_____

_____

Going forward, which of the following futures do you intend for yourself? Initial the mindset you choose for yourself:

_ _ _ _ _ _ **The path of stagnation:** It's a waste of time to spend time thinking about myself. I'm grown; I've got my education. I pretty much know myself already. I ought to just get on with it. All this self-awareness stuff is just avoidance of dealing with real life.

_ _ _ _ _ _ **The path of growth:** The kind of life I'll create is up to me, and I have to know who I am to do this well. I'm not going to just react my way through life and hope for the best. I want to learn why I respond as I do. I actively choose self-discovery as a way to make my life ever more meaningful and productive and my relationships livelier and fresher.

Contemplating each path, how do you feel? _____

_____

_____

_____

State here why you chose the path you did: _____

_____

_____

_____

Now imagine your higher self applauding all the time you've spent getting to know yourself today. It's standing up, clapping, and whistling. What might it be saying to you about the importance of your increased self-awareness?

_____

_____

_____

_____

_____

_____

_____

_____

_____

_____

_____

Sometimes there's a hidden benefit or learning embedded in some of our most difficult experiences. Do you think your parents' lack of interest in your inner experience paradoxically might have contributed to developing certain positive qualities in you?

For instance, which behaviors in EI adults did you dislike, making you resolve not to be like them when you grew up?

_____

_____

_____

_____

_____

_____

Describe any ways that their insensitive behavior toward you as you were growing up might have made you more self-aware and empathic.

_____

_____

_____

_____

_____

_____

_____

PART 2

Revive Your Self-Confidence

*With a healthy self-concept, you are not obsessed
with correcting what's wrong with you. You're just
trying to fulfill your potential and become genuinely
yourself. You have a healthy self-concept when your
individuality is precious to you, and you don't want
to be anybody or anything other than who you are.*

—Recovering from Emotionally Immature Parents (p. 174)

You need self-confidence for everything you attempt in life. Unfortunately, EI parents often undermine their children's self-confidence by being critical, envious, or disinterested. However, once you see how your self-confidence may have been wounded, you can nurse it back to health. It's tremendously relieving when you realize that your insecure feelings about your abilities might be EIP-based, not reality-based.

Tell me about a time in childhood when you spontaneously told someone something and they made you feel strange, wrong, or inappropriate. What was the occasion, setting, and how did you feel inside after they did that?

Tell me how this incident affected your self-confidence about freely expressing yourself.

Notice the voice inside you that undermines your trust in yourself and stirs up self-doubt. Tell it that's just fear and negativity, and ask it to leave you alone.

Self-doubt may still affect your spontaneity in your adult life. Let's finish this sentence: *I get self-conscious because I'm concerned they'll think* _____

_____

_____

_____

_____

    For the next two questions, imagine that I went back in time and interviewed your parents. Write down what first comes to mind. You may realize that your parents *never* addressed this issue with you. If so, write that down too. What they didn't do is as important as what they did.

If I asked your mother how she helped you build your self-confidence, what might she tell me?

_____

_____

_____

_____

If I asked your father how he supported your self-confidence, what might he say?

_____

_____

_____

_____

Looking back, how do you think your parents' attitude toward you affected the development of your self-confidence?

Who else in your life besides your parents undermined your confidence, and how did they do it?

In what *nonverbal* ways did people in your life undermine your self-confidence?

Pretend you're doing a home visit to observe yourself as a child in your family. What do you notice about this kid? What is it like for this child trying to develop self-confidence in this home? Describe that child as you take notes as an observer (using "she was"/"he was"/"they were").

_____

_____

_____

_____

_____

_____

_____

_____

Think about an important teacher or other person in your life who lifted your self-confidence. What did they do that emboldened you to follow your dreams?

_____

_____

_____

_____

_____

Let's look at times when you feel especially self-confident, as well as times when you still lack confidence:

I feel very confident that I am capable of _____

_____

_____

_____

_____

I have self-doubts and still struggle to feel confident when _____

_____

_____

_____

_____

_____

Self-confidence isn't bestowed by other people's reactions. How do you maintain your own self-confidence?

Think about how your self-confidence may have fluctuated recently. Jot down the things you said to yourself that either weakened you or made you stronger.

Listening to my internal dialogue, I see that I tear myself down by _____

When I remember the following kinds of things about myself, it raises my confidence:

Don't pressure yourself. Self-confidence is the work of a lifetime.

Read the following empowering statement out loud: *I have the right to be self-confident and to put time and effort into building my confidence*. If you want to claim this statement as a guiding reminder for the future, say it out loud and then copy it down with intention here:

_____

_____

_____

_____

Self-confidence is not arrogance.

Stand up for yourself when your EIP (or their voice inside your head) says: *You don't want to be too confident. No one will like you if you get all full of yourself.* Forcefully talk back to this attempt to dismiss your need to strengthen your self-confidence. (As always, you're writing for your eyes only.)

_____

_____

_____

It's up to you to believe in yourself and feel confident about what you can do in life.

Time to talk back and ask some impertinent questions of anyone—whether a real person or that voice in your head—who tries to undermine your confidence. Mentally defend your self-confidence by completing these prompts:

I want to know what gives you the right to _____

_____ .

What? Who says I can't _____

_____ ?

How come you get to _____

and I'm not supposed to _____ ?

Increase your confidence by completing the following strengthening thoughts.

From now on, nobody gets to _____

_____ .

It's my duty to get to feel confident so I can _____

_____ .

You can't make me _____

_____ .

· ·

Don't wait until you succeed before you feel confident. You won't need it then. Instead, practice feeling confident now.

· ·

Why do you think having more self-confidence would be good for you? What could you accomplish if you were more self-confident? Think about it for a minute, then do your best to convince me.

How do you feel about what you've journaled on self-confidence so far?

Going forward, which of the following paths appeals to you? Initial the mindset you now choose for yourself:

_____ **The path of stagnation:** I don't want to be one of those over-confident people that others envy. I had enough confidence to get where I am today. Why rock the boat and attempt new things I might fail at? I do well enough. If something big came along, I would work on my self-confidence then. But really, how likely is that to happen?

_____ **The path of growth:** We never know what life is going to throw at us. If I keep building my skills and self-knowledge now, I will have confidence to pursue good opportunities or challenges that come my way. I feel confident in my ability to change and build new skills. I want to build my self-confidence to the point where I try new things happily and don't fear others' reactions.

Contemplating each path, how do you feel? _____

_____

_____

_____

_____

State here why you chose the path you did: _____

_____

_____

_____

_____

Imagine your higher self listening in, encouraging you to build your self-confidence. It's thrilled by your change of attitude. Write down what you imagine it's saying to you about the importance of diminishing self-doubts and practicing more self-confidence.

Could there have been a benefit from losing your confidence at times? Is it possible that early blows to your self-confidence paradoxically might've increased your drive to make something of yourself? Tell me what you think.

Tell me about a time when someone tried to make you doubt yourself, but it just made you more determined to succeed.

_____

_____

_____

_____

_____

_____

_____

_____

What have you become as an adult that might have really surprised your parents' expectations for you as a kid?

_____

_____

_____

_____

_____

_____

_____

_____

PART 3

Build Your Sense of Belonging

Fortunately, once you start listening to your emotions instead of shutting them down, they will guide you toward an authentic connection with others. Knowing the cause of your emotional loneliness is the first step toward finding more fulfilling relationships.

—*Adult Children of Emotionally Immature Parents* (p. 10)

It's a special feeling to be with people who make us feel like we belong. However, it's hard to have a sense of belonging when you don't feel that people "get" you. This can lead to emotional loneliness and a feeling that you haven't yet found the place where you belong.

As an adult, before you can truly feel like you belong anywhere, you first have to accept and honor your own individuality. Both your self-awareness and your *willingness to be known* are foundational for your sense of belonging. Most people feel like an outsider when joining a new group, but it's even worse if you put on a façade for fear of exclusion. If you know yourself and accept your true nature, you will feel more comfortable letting yourself be known. Your sense of genuine belonging will flourish, the more authentic and transparent you are.

You can't feel like you truly belong if the people around you aren't interested in who you really are inside.

Tell me about a time when you innocently and spontaneously assumed you would be welcomed by others and then someone made you feel you didn't belong. What was the situation and how did you react inside to their rejection?

Tell me how this incident affected your sense of belonging, self-confidence, and self-acceptance.

Did incidents like this make you feel emotionally unsafe about joining new groups? If so, what kind of response do you most fear now from people?

I fear they might think I am _____

Once again, imagine that I went back in time and interviewed your parents. Write down what first comes to mind.

If I asked your mother how she tried to give you a sense of belonging, what might she say? _____

If I asked your father how he tried to make you feel included, what might he say?

Looking back, how do you think their attitude toward you affected the development of your sense of belonging?

Your social image of yourself may be affected by how much you felt you belonged in your family and in early social groups.

Maybe other people affected your sense of belonging when you were growing up. Who else besides your parents may have undermined your feelings of belonging, and how did they do that?

Who in your life made you feel welcomed and showed delight in having you with them?

_____

_____

_____

What did each of these types of people teach you about yourself?

_____

_____

_____

_____

_____

_____

_____

Check which of the following responses undermined your sense of belonging early in life:

- ☐ Someone actively rejected you or made it clear that you didn't belong with the rest of their group.

- ☐ They didn't reject you, but neither did they actively try to make you feel included as a welcomed member of the group.

- ☐ Someone made you feel different; you were with the group but didn't feel a part of the group.

Give it some thought and describe the *nonverbal* ways other people have undermined your sense of belonging (for example, looks, body language, tone).

Tell me how your feelings of belonging (or not belonging) affect how you feel about yourself.

Next, let's step back and once again imagine yourself as a child in your family. See yourself as a kid, and write about what it was like for that child when other people didn't try to make them feel that they belonged. From the perspective of an observer, write down your observations about yourself as a child, using the third person ("she was"/"he was"/"they were").

If you could go back in time, what would you want to tell that little kid?

Now describe the kind of situations where you still struggle to feel like you belong.

I still feel out of place in situations where _____

_____

_____

When someone makes us feel self-conscious or insecure, we instinctively hide our true self. Describe the kind of person you keep your distance from and tend to keep up a façade around.

_____

_____

_____

_____

_____

_____

_____

Write down three discouraging criticisms that the self-defeating voice in your head tells you when you don't feel like you belong:

1. _____

2. _____

3. _____

Now, refute each one and counter it with a more accurate statement.

1. _____

2. _____

3. _____

Let's explore how your own thoughts sometimes may make you feel excluded.

I have a harder time feeling like I belong when I'm thinking that _____

_____

_____

_____

_____

I strengthen my sense of belonging when I'm thinking that _____

_____

_____

_____

_____

What have you realized so far about the types of situations that are most likely to make you feel you *don't* belong? _____

_____

_____

_____

When you have that feeling, what reactions or behaviors of yours probably make things worse?

Now describe the ideal kind of situations or activities that *do* make you feel comfortable and like you belong:

And they give you that feeling because:

Think about someone in your life who made you feel welcome and like you belonged in their world. How did they relate to you so that you had a sense of belonging around them?

_____

_____

_____

_____

_____

How do you think this affected your life? _____

_____

_____

Where do you feel that secure sense of belonging now?

I feel like I belong in situations where _____

_____

_____

_____

_____

. . . .

What do you think it is about how you interact with people that strengthens your sense of belonging?

. . . .

47

Try on this empowering statement for yourself: *I have the right to feel included, and I can look for places where I can belong.* If you want to claim this self-affirming belief for your future, say it out loud and then copy it down with intention here:

_____

_____

_____

Remember a time when you really enjoyed talking to someone you didn't know well. What sort of people do you find most interesting and enjoyable?

_____

_____

_____

_____

Knowing where you feel most yourself supports your authenticity.

You're an adult now and you can actively choose where you want to fit in. Let's think of some impertinent things you can think to yourself if EIPs pressure you to enjoy activities or people you don't like:

Why should I _____?

Excuse me, but who says I have to _____?

How come I'm supposed to _____

_____

instead of doing what I really enjoy, like _____?

Not only do you have the right to challenge pushy EI ideas about where you *should* want to belong, you can also clarify where you *do* belong by using these strengthening thoughts:

*From now on, the kind of groups I want to belong to will be*_____

_____.

I plan to let people get to know me more by _____

_____.

I will no longer force myself to _____

_____.

If you're not accepting toward yourself, it will be hard for anyone else to welcome the real you. Write a transparent, authentic description of who you really are, as if you're informing other people what they would get from getting to know you and from having you in their group. Describe why you would be a much-needed addition to their group.

_____

_____

_____

_____

_____

_____

_____

You have the right to seek out people who make you feel comfortable and included.

A quick check-in: How do you feel so far about your journaling on this section about belonging?

_____

_____

_____

_____

_____

To be comfortable in a group, you first have to get comfortable with yourself.

If you had to choose the best path forward, which appeals to you more? Initial the mindset you now choose for yourself:

_____ **The path of stagnation:** It's up to others whether I belong or not. I'd better wait and see how they feel about me before I make overtures or try to participate in the group. And what if I ultimately decide I don't like this group? Then I'll be stuck with people I don't want to be around. Worse, what if they decide to reject me from the group? Trying to belong has no guarantees; I'm not sure I want to try.

_____ **The path of growth:** If I want other people to like and welcome me, I need to know and accept myself just as I am. I will be honest with myself and transparent with other people. I won't try to belong to any group I don't want to spend time with or don't feel welcomed into. If I want to belong, I will ask to participate, get to know the people, and see if I feel like I belong there. If after I make these efforts, it isn't working or things change, I'll try another group until I find one that feels easier to belong to.

Contemplating each path, how do you feel? _____

_____

_____

_____

State here why you chose the path you did: _____

_____

_____

_____

Imagine your higher self listening in, celebrating the way you've figured out what you need to feel like you belong. It's cheering you on, with a huge smile on its face. Imagine what your higher self would say to you about your decision to be yourself, to be more transparent, and to build a true sense of belonging by letting people get to know the real you.

_____

_____

_____

_____

_____

_____

Is it possible that early feelings of not belonging may have paradoxically increased your ability to be independent and find your own way? Did early experiences make you extra appreciative now of groups where you do feel accepted and recognized?

Tell me about a time when you initially didn't feel like you belonged, but you learned to fit in anyway.

_____

_____

_____

_____

_____

_____

Write about a time when you felt fine about not belonging, because you knew you didn't fit in with this group of people.

_____

_____

_____

_____

What relationships have you been a part of as an adult that might have been very different from your parents' expectations of you as a kid?

PART 4

Look Out for Yourself and Set Boundaries

Emotionally sensitive and empathic people who were raised by an EI parent can find it hard to set boundaries. Caring about other people's feelings often leads to feeling guilty for establishing limits. You might worry that saying no will make you appear unkind, selfish, or even rejecting. You don't want anyone to feel bad.

—*Self-Care for Adult Children of Emotionally Immature Parents* (p. 27)

EIPs see themselves as good people, so to them it's absurd for you to say you want limits on their behavior. Because EIPs' worldview is always self-justifying, they feel sure they are innocent of whatever it is you think they're doing to you. Can't you see that they're just kidding, that they're just offering a sensible suggestion, or that they are just being a loving, concerned parent or person? They can't understand why you are being so negative. Why would you need to set limits with them when the relationship is working just fine as far as they're concerned? When you set a boundary with them, they think you're saying they're a bad *person*.

For EI parents, harmony between parent and adult child *means* blurred boundaries. Getting along means accepting unsolicited advice and expectations that you will go along with whatever they want. Interacting like that means that you care about each other—that you're family, that you're *close*.

EIPs think their needs are far more important than your right to know what you want.

EIPs believe that any attempt toward self-protection or setting boundaries is unloving and disrespectful. EIPs can make you feel guilty and selfish for not rubber-stamping everything they want. Their conviction of their infallibility requires that you split yourself in two: one part to go along with them and one part to feel what you really feel. Essentially, their message to you is: *You should suppress your true wishes so I can continue to approve of you and we can be close.*

When EI parents disapprove of their adult child's choices, it would never occur to them to question themselves or try to understand what their adult child wants and needs for their own life. Why would they do that when they already know they're right? They don't see that their certainty mindset is exactly what you need protection from. You have rights as a person too.

You need boundaries with anyone who acts like they know better what's good for you than you do.

In this part about self-protection, you'll journal about three ways that EIPs can affect your ability to protect yourself and set necessary boundaries:

- How they can affect your instinct for self-preservation
- What makes it hard to set limits on them in the moment
- How they confuse you when you try to hold them responsible for their behavior

Sometimes a person's inability to set boundaries or protect themselves is caused by traumatic memories. Our goal here is not to uncover trauma or trigger unmanageable distress, so if you need to, be selective about answering these prompts. If any questions make you uncomfortable, please skip them and go on. There are plenty of other prompts to choose from.

Tell me about a time growing up when you were not allowed to protect yourself or set boundaries.

You might have learned that accepting other people's control is the easiest way to be seen as a good person.

In what ways did this affect your ability to protect yourself as an adult?

For the next two questions, write down what first comes to mind. Remember, it's still important if they *didn't* do these things.

If I asked your mother how she helped you learn to protect yourself and set boundaries, what might she say?

If I asked your father how he helped you learn to protect yourself with limits and boundaries, what might he say?

Tell me how your parents made you feel as a child when you tried to stand up for yourself or set a boundary with them.

_____

_____

_____

_____

Recall a time when you objected to what they wanted you to do. How did they react?

_____

_____

_____

_____

How did your parents communicate _nonverbally_ that they thought you were not entitled to state your preferences or limits?

_____

_____

_____

_____

_____

Who else in your life taught you to put up with things and not complain or set limits? How did they get you to accept that?

_____

_____

_____

_____

_____

_____

Describe an incident in which you learned that giving in and not caring was easier than speaking up or flatly refusing.

_____

_____

_____

_____

_____

· · · · · · ·

Following someone's lead and suppressing how you really feel is not a solution; it's a capitulation.

· · · · · · ·

What kind of reactions will make you back down the quickest, even when you really want to disagree or set a boundary?

_____

_____

_____

_____

_____

Imagine observing yourself as a child in need of self-protective boundaries. Describe what you see. Does this little kid act like they have a right to their preferences and boundaries? Assume a journalistic distance and write about yourself as this child, using the third person ("she was"/"he was"/"they were").

_____

_____

_____

_____

_____

_____

_____

_____

_____

Who in your life made you feel safe to tell them your preferences and to say no if you needed to? How did they give you that feeling?

How would you describe your current overall ability to protect your boundaries and set limits with people?

Below, write about times when you were either happy with or regretful about your efforts at self-preservation or setting boundaries:

I'm proud of the time when I protected myself and set a limit on

I was disappointed with myself when I didn't protect myself or set a limit when

What is the most effective way someone can usually make you back down?

_____

_____

_____

_____

_____

_____

Think of a time when you felt unsure about standing up for yourself and setting boundaries with someone. What did the inner opposing sides of yourself have to say and why?

TAKE A STAND	LET IT GO

63

Think of a time when you stood up for yourself in a way you liked, or when you set a boundary and felt calm and good about it. How would you describe your state of mind at the time? What do you think enabled you to stand up for yourself like that?

Make the case for why you are entitled to protect yourself, say no, and set limits, even if the other person doesn't like it:

Would you like to claim the following empowering belief for the future?

I have the right to protect myself as needed and to set limits on other people's behavior toward me. If you would like to own this position, say it out loud and then copy it down here with intention:

_____

_____

_____

_____

Now just for fun, let's think of some impertinent things that you could've said to EIPs in the past when they objected to your self-protection and boundaries:

What gives you the right to _____?

Hold on, who says I can't _____?

How come you get to _____

and I'm not allowed to _____?

Now let's practice audaciously setting boundaries with any person or inner belief that tries to coerce you. You might think, *Audaciously?* Well, yes, it can feel that way, but it's really your right.

From now on, you don't get to _____.

It's my duty to protect myself so I can _____.

Nobody has the right to make me _____.

Spell out why thinking of your own self-preservation first is a necessity. Why is protecting yourself and setting boundaries especially crucial for you? Do your best to convince me.

A quick check-in: How do you feel about your journaling on this section so far?

Time doesn't let us stand still. Think about the direction you're headed for. Initial the mindset you are now choosing for yourself:

_ _ _ _ _ _ **The path of stagnation:** It's not worth it to cause a problem when I don't want to go along with something. With these people, it's easier to go along to get along. I don't see them that often. It would be mean of me to tell them no when they care so much about this issue. I'll do what I want the rest of the time.

_ _ _ _ _ _ **The path of growth:** Every time I don't speak up when I feel strongly about a boundary, I am setting myself up for emotional exhaustion and passive resentment. I can't have a real relationship with someone if I let them call all the shots. I set boundaries because it keeps our relationship honest and real. I have just as much right to my limits as they do to theirs.

Contemplating each path, how do you feel? _____

_____

_____

_____

_____

State here why you chose the path you did: _____

_____

_____

_____

_____

Sit back and imagine yourself in the future, able to protect your interests easily and set clear boundaries in your relationships. Inhabit that vision of yourself and then describe what it would feel like:

Imagine your higher self being excited that you are pursuing this new future. It's giving you the thumbs-up and is thrilled that you're going to start protecting yourself. What would it say to you right now?

Looking back, do you think you might have learned anything useful from *not* being allowed to speak up or to set boundaries? For instance, I wonder if you developed any of the following skills. Please check the ones that apply to you:

- ☐ Did you learn how to be super-tactful so that other people wouldn't be upset by your boundaries or opinions?
- ☐ Can you instantly tell when a topic is starting to make someone defensive?
- ☐ Can you easily predict which people are going to be hard to set a boundary with?

How have these sensitivities helped you in your adult life at times?

_____

_____

_____

_____

_____

_____

_____

_____

_____

_____

PART 5

Respond in the Moment

Every time you speak up—in whatever uncomfortable or hesitant way you can manage to do it—you bring about more meaningful communication and pull the relationship out of stagnating in superficiality.

—Recovering from Emotionally Immature Parents (p. 186)

Many times, your best chance at setting a limit is in the moment. Speaking up and stating a boundary is easiest as soon as an issue arises. However, an EIP's judgmental, quick-draw attitude can have a chilling effect on your immediate response. You may freeze, feel immobilized, fear their reaction, or be unsure of your right to say no. Your stunned moment of indecision is all they need to take over and direct what you do. EIPs often get their way by dumbfounding you with their illogical, tangential, or even absurd responses, delivered as if they were above reproach. It's easy to feel immobilized and overwhelmed by their brain-scrambling responses at times. Once you get confused, you can lose touch with your true desires and feelings, and forget to protest or stand your ground.

When you hesitate, they dominate.

Describe a time when you felt overwhelmed by an EIP's upset reaction and couldn't speak up or keep to your boundary:

_____

_____

_____

_____

_____

_____

_____

How did you feel about yourself and your response in this situation?

_____

_____

_____

_____

_____

_____
　　　　　　　　　　　　　　　　　　　　　　　　　
_____
　　　　　　　　　　　　　　　　　　　　　　　　　
_____

> *Not speaking up is not a sign of weakness; it's a sign of intimidation.*

For the next two questions, write down what first comes to mind, whether your parents helped you with this or not.

If I asked your mother how she helped you learn to stand up for yourself right away, what might she say?

_____

_____

_____

If I asked your father how he helped you stand up for yourself as soon as someone tried to push you around, what might he say?

_____

_____

_____

Tell me about a person in your past who had an inhibiting effect on your ability to instinctively and immediately protect your boundaries:

How did they intimidate you or throw you off-balance so that you became frozen like a deer in the headlights, unable to respond in your own defense?

Go back in time and watch yourself from a distance as a child who is caught off guard and feels stunned by an older person's reaction. Describe how this child looks in the moment, and how you feel seeing them be afraid or confused:

Who in your life made you feel empowered to *resist* domination or intimidation? How did they make you feel justified in immediately standing up for yourself?

_____

_____

_____

_____

_____

_____

How would you like to respond when it comes to reacting to pushy people in the moment? Describe your ideal version of how you would like to deal with such situations.

_____

_____

_____

_____

_____

_____

We don't have to be aggressive or tough when we speak up; all we have to do is hold on to our own point of view.

What were you taught that undermined your ability to respond self-protectively and declare your limits in the moment?

Write down three things that the self-defeating voice in your head says to stop you from standing up for yourself:

1.

2.

3.

What would you like to think instead? What would you need to believe in your bones in order to react in the moment to take care of yourself and assert your boundaries?

_____

_____

_____

_____

Let's practice imagining some impertinent thoughts toward anyone who tries to intimidate or pressure you into going along with what they want:

Hang on, what gives you the right to _____ ?

Who says I can't _____ ?

How come you get to _____

and yet I'm not supposed to _____ ?

Now, by finishing these next statements, audaciously claim your right to respond in the moment:

From now on, you don't have my permission to _____

_____ .

If you try to dominate or control me, I have the right to react immediately by

_____

I'm on to you. You can't make me feel _____

_____ *anymore.*

Write a letter of self-acceptance to yourself, showing compassionate under-standing of how intimidating some people can be and why it has been so hard for you to speak up to set limits in the moment. You can reread this letter for support in the future whenever you find it difficult to assert yourself.

A quick check-in: How do you feel so far about journaling on your ability to respond by speaking up right away?

Review and contemplate your progress so far in being able to shake off intimidation and defend yourself when an EIP is trying to shut you down. Tell me what you have felt good about doing, even if in tiny steps:

_____

_____

_____

_____

_____

_____

As long as you don't disconnect from yourself, you can't get confused.

Which one of the following paths would you like to go down? Initial the one that best signals your intent:

_____ **The path of stagnation:** There's no way I can ever stand up to their criticism, contempt, or anger. They make me speechless. I'm just going to keep trying to not make waves, and then I'll do what I feel like once I get away from them. Frankly, they scare me and I'm no match for them.

_____ **The path of growth:** I'm done granting them the power to intimidate and confuse me when I stand up for myself. I'm going to start getting prepared in advance so they can't dominate me through destabilizing me. When they confuse or ridicule me, I'm going to keep a grip on my own opinion and stand my ground. I don't have to convince them; I just have to stay connected to myself and my own point of view. I can certainly do that.

Contemplating each path, how do you feel?

_____

_____

_____

State here why you chose the path you did:

_____

_____

_____

Take a moment and picture yourself in the future. Imagine a situation where you typically feel overwhelmed or shut down by someone, and now imagine that you aren't confused by them or impressed by their ego, and you keep your own point of view. You don't lose yourself or get muddleheaded when the EIP goes off on a tangent and makes you freeze up in confusion and self-doubt. You remain calm and clear about your preferences and position. Imagine what it would feel like to speak up, or even just to disagree secretly and silently (that counts too). Describe how you would feel if you accessed that self-possessed, determined state.

_____

_____

_____

_____

Your higher self is so happy that you're no longer letting them paralyze or befuddle you. What does this higher self want to say to you about your intention to keep your wits about you when EIPs try to intimidate or confuse you into submission?

_____

_____

_____

_____

_____

I wonder if you think anything good has come from feeling overpowered or stunned in the face of someone's domination. How has your occasional inability to react quickly or speak up actually served you well in a situation? Describe how your passive, shocked response was a good thing in a moment when it would've made things worse to react?

_____

_____

_____

_____

_____

_____

PART 6

End Self-Blame

When you find yourself doubting reality and blaming yourself, that's your cue to step back and question why you feel guilty. Perhaps you have an inner child part of you that feels guilty whenever someone seems unhappy. You can't let that confused, guilty child part run your life. You can understand the guilt, but you don't have to accept it. Challenge that self-blame reflex. You, the adult, are running the show, not your guilt-ridden child part from long ago.

—Disentangling from Emotionally Immature People (p. 109)

EIPs feel entitled to take control of most interactions. Since they lack the imagination or empathy to sense others' experiences, they don't consider how their actions may affect someone else. Without adequate self-reflection, EIPs don't take responsibility for their behavior and will defensively blame others if confronted. As a result, you will be the one expected to feel guilt, shame, and responsibility for any problems in the relationship.

EIPs are sure they're doing what's best for everybody.

You have to be careful not to accept unwarranted guilt, blame, or responsibility in your interactions with EIPs. You may need to protect yourself not only from their blame-casting but also against your *own* tendency to scrutinize yourself for the tiniest bit of guilt in the situation.

Ask yourself whether, in a conflictual situation, you think first about what *you* may have done wrong, and tend to give others the benefit of the doubt. Tell me about a time when you did this.

_____

_____

_____

_____

_____

Because internalizer ACEIPs are so self-reflective, they try to be scrupulously fair by taking part of the blame, even if it wasn't their fault.

What does it feel like to sink into guilt, shame, fear, or self-doubt instead of standing up for yourself?

_____

_____

_____

_____

_____

_____

_____

Tell me about a time when you felt you _had_ to give in to an emotional coercion or emotional takeover (that is, by treating an EIP's emotional upset like a real emergency, even at a cost to yourself.)

_____

_____

_____

_____

_____

_____

_____

What kinds of emotional reactions (verbal and nonverbal) from others will make you feel guilt and shame the fastest?

What types of criticism or accusations work best to make you take responsibility for other people's unpleasant behavior toward you?

Picture yourself as a child who is feeling remorse or guilt for upsetting someone by speaking up or drawing a boundary. What feelings come up in you as you see this child feel bad about a situation that wasn't their fault?

Do you tend to feel overly guilty or excessively responsible? Tell me about a time when you took on too much responsibility for someone else's feelings.

How would you like to feel instead whenever someone tries to make you feel bad for not giving in to what they want?

_____

_____

_____

_____

_____

_____

What if you couldn't feel guilt or shame? How would you respond to unfair accusations or criticisms?

_____

_____

_____

_____

_____

_____

Describe how you will look at future situations so you can stay self-possessed, resist automatic guilt, and be clear about who has responsibility for what.

Would you like to claim the following empowering belief? If so, say it out loud and then copy it down with intention here: *I refuse to take responsibility or feel guilty for a situation if I really wasn't to blame.*

Let's build even more confidence by completing and saying out loud the following impertinent questions and audacious responses to being "guilted" by someone.

Nobody gives you the right to _____.

Who says I have to _____?

How come I have to _____
but you don't?

The next time you expect me to feel guilty, I'm going to remember that _____
_____.

I no longer agree to feel _____ *every time you*
_____.

It's essential for my emotional self-preservation for me not to _____
_____.

Now let's summarize why you think it's important for you to stop taking too much responsibility for other people's negative behavior.

_____
_____
_____
_____
_____

*EIPs are sure their needs
are innocent and justified,
so they deny they've
ever been overbearing,
disrespectful, or hurtful.*

Going forward, which of the following paths do you want to commit to? Initial the one that best describes your choice:

_ _ _ _ _ _   **The path of stagnation:** I can manage to get along with difficult people by disconnecting from myself and my preferences. I avoid fights by not saying how much things bother me. I remind myself that it doesn't make any difference what I do; they will have the last word and make things even more difficult for me. It's easier just to go along and say I'm sorry.

_ _ _ _ _ _   **The path of growth:** I am very bothered by people treating me poorly. I feel a natural indignation and urge to protect my position. I may be tempted to go along with things to make life easier, but then I compute the expensive long-term consequences of not putting a stop to this right now. I hate conflict but I'm willing to state my preferences and put up with their grief, just so I don't have to regret it later. I accept that I could be mistaken at times, but I refuse to feel guilty for respectfully stating my own point of view.

Contemplating each path, how do you feel?

State here why you chose the path you did: _____

_____

_____

_____

What would be a good way to describe how you've evolved in your right to protect yourself and not feel guilty? Don't overthink it; just let the answer pop into your mind.

I used to be a _____

_____ ,

but now I'm more of a _____

_____ .

Has there been any upside to worrying about whether you were to blame for other people's distress? Has it helped you in your life to consider whether you might be at fault, or might partly bear responsibility for a conflict? If so, describe how:

_____

_____

_____

_____

_____

_____

Imagine that you now live your life as an active responder who doesn't avoid politely voicing your preferences and boundaries. Describe how your life would change if you started courteously saying what you believe, what you want or don't want, even if it upset or angered other people. How does it feel inside to be proud of your emotionally self-protective behavior every day? How does it feel to wake up each morning knowing that you won't be going along with anything that day that doesn't feel right or goes against what you prefer?

PART 7

Listen to Yourself to Empower Yourself

*Once you see yourself as equal in importance—
in spite of their behavior to the contrary—you'll
naturally think of more active and assertive
responses. You'll ask for what you prefer in the
moment. You'll respond in ways that gently remind
them: "I'm here too and my needs matter as much
as yours." You'll explain what would be best for you
without shame or apology because there's nothing
shameful about being on an equal footing.*

—Recovering from Emotionally Immature Parents (pp. 180–181)

EI parents don't think much about their children's thoughts and feelings, so they usually don't notice their children's emotional and psychological experiences. Consequently, their children get the impression that what they feel inside is not important and certainly has little influence over what the parents do. If the grown-ups don't listen to you, you learn not to listen to yourself.

Listening to yourself is vital for believing in what you're doing. It also supports the self-care you need to stay healthy and adequately energetic. Your inner guidance helps you feel connected to your own power and can provide important insight from your body about what's bothering you.

Admittedly, it *does* make it easier to get along with EIPs when you tune out your own inner guidance. As a result, many ACEIPs learn to discount their feelings and intuitions, not trusting themselves to have good ideas or sound instincts. When you don't believe you can trust your inner experiences, you stop defending your right to have your own point of view.

When you don't listen to yourself or trust your feelings, indecision and a lack of clear goals quickly follow.

What is your gut response to the idea of more empowerment and entitlement for yourself? Does it give you a thrill of self-sufficiency? Or does it make you shrink back a little, like it's too egotistical?

_____

_____

_____

_____

_____

I think you should feel emboldened to be a free adult, to take good care of yourself, and to feel entitled to live your own life. You can't function well as an adult if you don't feel empowered and entitled to go after the best life for you.

Let's explore how well you listen to yourself and how justified you feel in taking good care of yourself as an adult.

First, let's consider how the EIPs in your life may have impacted your sense of entitlement to self-care. Put a check next to any of the following statements that fit the feelings you have:

☐ It seems that other people have rights, while I have duties and obligations.

☐ I feel bad if I don't prioritize what would make others more comfortable, even if it's at my expense.

☐ I do too much because I don't want anyone to think I'm lazy, selfish, or thoughtless.

☐ I worry about appearing egotistical if I include my wishes in a decision.

You've worked hard to become an adult. How do you feel about claiming your adult power?

What kind of messages did you get in childhood about being lazy, not doing enough work, or wasting time? How do you think those messages affected your self-image as an adult? How do they affect your ability to relax and enjoy time off?

_____

_____

_____

_____

For the next two questions, write down what first comes to mind. If your parent didn't offer this guidance, make a note of that too.

If I asked your mother how she taught you to listen to yourself, what might she say?

If I asked your father how he taught you to pay attention to your gut feelings, what might he say?

Think of people in your life who made you feel like it was okay to rest and take care of yourself. How did they show you that?

Although they freely do things for themselves, EIPs often act like your self-care decisions have disregarded them in a selfish way. To feel okay about listening to yourself, you have to remind yourself that your experiences and development matter.

Tell me about a time when someone made you feel selfish for taking your own needs into account.

Tell me about a time when you gave more than you wanted to. How did you feel afterward, physically and emotionally?

If you have ever felt entitled to ask for what you needed *without* feeling guilty about it, tell me what made it possible for you to listen to yourself that time.

Close your eyes and pretend you're observing yourself as a child who is being accused of selfishness, laziness, or thoughtlessness because you did what you wanted without thinking of others. Describe how that child looks and feels when they learned it was "bad" to have chosen what they really wanted to do.

How easy is it for you to listen to your body and intuition in order to take care of yourself? How do you respond to your own needs, especially for pleasure, rest, recreation, quiet time, or entertainment?

Thinking about pursuits that you really enjoy, which ones would you love to feel no guilt about pursuing and why?

_____

_____

_____

_____

_____

Make an argument for why you *should* take time to pursue an activity that relaxes and invigorates you.

_____

_____

_____

_____

How have you hurt yourself by not listening to your needs?

_____

_____

_____

_____

Write down three restorative experiences that the busy voice in your head tells you it's selfish to take time for:

1. _____

2. _____

3. _____

Try saying out loud, *I am entitled to listen to how I feel, so I will do something pleasant and entertaining for myself every day.* What is your honest internal reaction to hearing yourself saying these words? (You can further claim that empowering belief for your future by copying it down here with intent.)

_____

_____

_____

_____

Self-care and listening to yourself don't have to come at anybody's expense, except those people who want to dictate how you live.

If you were to plan any type of self-care, what experiences or activities would reinvigorate you most?

- _____   - _____

- _____   - _____

- _____   - _____

- _____   - _____

If you have a hard time taking care of yourself, try out these impertinent questions to challenge that voice in your head telling you to put everything else first in your life. Be sure to write down your first thoughts, without editing them:

How come I'm not supposed to _____ ?

Hold on a minute, why can't I _____ ?

I think of others all the time. It's about time I got to _____

_____ .

Now make your audacious claim to self-care by completing the following:

From now on, I'm going to _____ .

I have to take good care of myself and my energy because _____

_____ .

Nobody gets to tell me what I _____ .

Take a moment and check in on how you're feeling about this topic so far.

Close your eyes and imagine feeling good about taking care of yourself. Next, zoom ahead to ten years from now. Pretend you are looking back gratefully at the way you gave yourself the kind of breaks you really needed. Write a letter of appreciation to that younger you for finally listening to your needs.

Can you really live a happy life if you don't feel entitled to listen to yourself?

What would be a good way to describe your evolving attitude toward self-care? Write the first thing that pops into your mind.

I used to treat myself like a _____ ,

but now I see myself more like a _____ .

If you learned not to listen to your needs or take care of yourself, what good things may have come from that nevertheless? Has believing that putting yourself first is selfish contributed anything positive to your life? Were there any times when suppressing or delaying your needs paid off for you later in life?

EIPs imply that self-empowerment is legitimate for them, but morally questionable for you.

_____

_____

_____

_____

_____

_____

_____

_____

_____

_____

_____

For the next two questions, write down what first comes to mind, whether your parent engaged in this behavior or not.

If I asked your mother how she helped you listen to yourself, what might she say?

_____

_____

_____

_____

If I asked your father how he helped you pay attention to your intuition and self-awareness, what might he say?

_____

_____

_____

_____

Pretend you are looking at yourself as a child in a moment when that child was feeling optimistic and powerful. How do you see other people reacting to this child's sense of empowerment? How does it make _you_ feel to see this child so connected to themselves?

_____

_____

_____

_____

Write about whether you feel empowered to be yourself as an adult. Are you listening to yourself, exerting your power, and expressing your own preferences in the world? Describe your style of asserting yourself, such as when you ask for what you want or defend your beliefs when necessary.

In which kinds of situations do you trust and listen to yourself most easily?

When do you have *no* trouble stating what you need?

Read the following empowering statement, and if you agree, say it out loud and copy it down with intention as a guiding belief for the future:

I am entitled to feel vigorous, powerful, and bold. I'm not threatening anyone with those feelings. I'm listening to my desires and goals. There is absolutely nothing wrong with knowing what I want out of life.

_____

_____

_____

_____

_____

To prepare for people who will question your right to listen to yourself, try out these impertinent thoughts. (You don't have to *say* these to anybody, but you can *think* them.) Write the first thing that pops into your mind:

Why do you try to tell me what to think, when the truth is _____

_____ ?

When I listen to myself and feel my power, are you afraid that _____

_____ ?

When you tell me to listen to you instead of myself, I _____

_____ .

To feel empowered by listening to yourself and acting on the things you want to do in life, complete these audacious, strengthening responses toward your EIPs' attempts at control:

From now on, you don't get to _____ .

I've decided to become the kind of person who _____

_____ .

You don't intimidate me anymore because _____

_____ .

I'd love for you to explain to me now why you *should* listen to yourself and assert your right to exert the power of personal choice in your life, regardless of anyone's approval or disapproval.

_____

_____

_____

_____

_____

_____

_____

_____

_____

_____

How do you feel about writing on this topic so far?

Every day we choose which road we are going to take forward in our lives. Initial the path you intend to take right now.

_____ **The path of stagnation:** I don't want to make anybody mad or hurt their feelings by standing up for my choices. I don't like entitled people and don't want to be one of them. I suppress my needs for self-care so I don't seem lazy or selfish to others. I refrain from feeling my power in any situation because I may offend someone and cause them to criticize or embarrass me. Who needs the stress?

_____ **The path of growth:** I listen to myself about what I need to feel my best. I empower myself to speak up in whatever polite way I can for my own rights, even when I sound tentative or unsure. The important thing for me is to go on record about what I think. I don't let other people assume that I will go along with whatever they say. My intuition guides me about what I'm genuinely entitled to. I claim my power when it's legitimate because nobody else is going to do it for me. Listening to myself in every situation gives me the happiest life I can have, with as few regrets as possible.

Contemplating each path, how do you feel? _____

_____

_____

_____

State here why you chose the path you did: _____

_____

_____

_____

Close your eyes and imagine what it would feel like to be entitled and empowered to listen to yourself and make your own choices. Now describe that feeling to me as if it's already happened and you're looking back gratefully to when you started to listen to yourself.

_____

_____

_____

_____

_____

_____

_____

_____

Think poetically. What would be a good metaphor for how you've changed since you started listening to yourself and taking care of yourself? Fill in the following:

I used to be a _____ ,

but now I'm more a _____ .

When did someone discouraging your dreams make you more determined?

_____

_____

_____

_____

_____

When others tried to disempower you or didn't listen to what you needed, what did you learn from the experience that made your life better as an adult?

_____

_____

_____

_____

See your higher self applauding your growth and progress. It is bursting with happiness over the way you are listening to yourself when making decisions in your life. Your higher self is joyful whenever you empower yourself by listening to your intuition and preferences. It's so delighted that you take care of yourself.

PART 8

Learn to Become Resilient

When you've grown up too fast, you may be shocked in adulthood by how overwhelmed you feel in the face of unforeseen problems. You try to be ready for anything, but an unexpected crisis can trigger childish desperation over having absolutely no idea what to do.

—*Disentangling from Emotionally Immature People* (p. 55)

EI parents inevitably do a poor job of showing their children how to cope with stress. These parents' unresolved emotional needs, judgmental thinking, and low stress tolerance make it hard for them to keep their emotional equilibrium when things aren't going well. Instead of their protecting and guiding you in childhood, those roles may have felt reversed at times. Growing up, you may have had to suppress your anxieties in order to give your parent *your* support.

EI parents have trouble manifesting the calm confidence that would have given you the childhood security of a *holding environment* (Winnicott 1989), a reassuring emotional atmosphere that nurtures security and growth. Adequately mature parents would have shown you how to withstand and regulate your intense childhood emotions within a secure parent-child bond. When you got upset and felt out of control, a mature enough parent would've known how to comfort you through your distress and wouldn't have panicked or needed you to stop. In other words, they wouldn't have been destabilized by your distress. They would've attended you through your childhood emotional storms so that you felt reassured and re-empowered. You could have painlessly acquired self-confidence and optimism, discovering that even when initially overwhelmed, you could still work your way through problems by getting help from others as needed.

But with an EI parent, you likely learned that you would end up feeling *worse* if you turned to them for help. You may have discovered a long time ago that your parent wouldn't respond to your problems with calm skill. Instead, you experienced your parent becoming reactive, tense, and critical—perhaps even angry with you. When your best option under such circumstances is to comfort *yourself*, you tend to build a personality that is robustly mature and capable on the outside, but with a squishy center of insecurity on the inside.

You learned that it was easier to shut down and ride it out alone, rather than to seek help from an overreactive parent.

You may seem to have it all together now: the person others turn to with their problems. Only you—or those very close to you—know how panicky or overwhelmed you can feel at times. As a child who often felt in over your head, you may adeptly bluff your way through challenges but without feeling real confidence. Even though what started out as a "false self" capable façade (Winnicott 1989) probably has evolved into real competence by now, your unprocessed emotional insecurity might make it hard to own who you have become. This lingering insecurity can result in *imposter syndrome*, that feeling when your adult reputation has surpassed how you see yourself on the inside (Clance 2017).

Having to cope by yourself too early in life can mean that when you don't instantly know what to do in adulthood, you may involuntarily reconnect with the feelings of that frightened, overwhelmed inner child who panics. Therefore, developing resilience means not only meeting the challenge but also attending to that unsupported child part within you (Schwartz 1995). Although you may still get those reverberations of fear and loneliness, your best path forward now is to empathize with that scared inner reaction and then deliberately turn it over to your capable adult self, who has learned how to figure out the next steps to take.

To summarize, there are three ways that an EI parent may have impacted your problem solving and resilience:

- The EI parent's stressed demeanor made you feel you should keep your needs to yourself and not ask for help.
- The EI parent's tendency to get worked up and blame others never showed you how to remain reasonable and objective while calmly working your way through complex challenges.
- The EI parent's impatience and criticism made it hard for you to accept and learn from your mistakes as you looked for solutions.

Now let's look at how all this may have played out in your life.

Are you ever embarrassed about how scared or hopeless you can feel at times? What it's like when you feel overwhelmed and can't imagine how things will ever turn out right?

_____

_____

_____

_____

Think about a time when you got past a problem and resolved the situation after some initial panic; did you go back and deal with the part of you that had been so scared? Or did you just move on and try to forget about those feelings? If you were to deal with this scared part later, what do you think would be a healing way to interact with it?

_____

_____

_____

_____   *Trying to forget your*
                                                             overwhelmed feelings after
_____   *the fear has passed sets*
                                                             you up for it to resurge in
_____   *the next crisis. Instead,*
                                                             acknowledge and empathize
_____   *with your fearful part so it*
                                                             can recover.

Growing up, did you feel free to ask for help? What did you expect would happen if you did?

_____

_____

_____

_____

Describe a time in childhood when things at home were overwhelmingly confusing, scary, or out of control. How did you cope with this situation?

_____

_____

_____

_____

_____

_____

_____

In what ways might you still be using this method?

_____

_____

_____

Now pretend you are an observer, watching the child you were during that difficult time. What stands out to you about that child? How do you feel as you watch their family environment unfold?

You may have experienced parent-child role reversal in childhood. In what ways were you relied on like a fellow adult, rather than a child in the family?

For the next two questions, write down what first comes to mind. If your parents didn't teach you these things, note that as well.

If I interviewed your mother about how she taught you to think about and deal with problems, what might she say?

_____

_____

_____

If I asked your father how he showed you what to do when you felt over-whelmed by a problem, what might he tell me?

_____

_____

_____

Sum up what you observed from the adults in your childhood about how to approach problems. How did each parent react to life's challenges when things didn't go their way or when problems became complex and frustrating?

_____

_____

_____

_____

_____

Who in your childhood world demonstrated the *least* effective or most self-defeating way of dealing with adversity? What was it about their style that you didn't admire?

EIPs' insistence on being right and their quickness to accuse others make them poor role models for handling stress.

_____

_____

_____

_____

_____

_____

_____

Which of their attitudes might you have picked up that could be interfering with your coping ability? Which attitudes would you now most like to change in yourself?

_____

_____

_____

_____

_____

_____

Picture the most capable person around you while you were growing up. How did they respond when things went wrong?

_____

_____

_____

_____

In your whole life, whose manner of coping have you admired the most? What was it about them that you'd like to copy?

_____

_____

_____

_____

Tell me about a comforting person in your life who helped you calm down and feel better in a difficult situation. What was it about the way they approached your problem that was the most helpful to you?

_____

_____

_____

_____

If someone had done a painting of you as a child during those times when you felt most lost, with no one to turn to who understood, fill in the following sentences about what that portrait would look like:

I see _____ .

They look _____ .

They seem to be feeling _____ .

That kid looks like they could use some _____ . *I feel*

_____ *when I see them.*

Tell me about a time in childhood when you had no choice but to tell someone about your problem and ask for help. How did that experience go for you?

_____

_____

_____

_____

_____

_____

_____

_____

_____

Now let's look at how you could deal with present-day difficulties as an adult. Instead of alternating between two incompatible parts of yourself—the overwhelmed child and the strong resourceful adult—bring them together in your imagination for a supportive interaction between the two (Jung 1997; Schwartz 1995). What does your scared child part say to your adult part? How does your adult part respond?

_____

_____

_____

_____

_____

_____

Think of a recent difficult situation that you dreaded. Let the overwhelmed child part of yourself tell you and me why it was so frightened (Schwartz 1995; Whitfield 1987).

_____

_____

_____

_____

_____

_____

Let's think of how you could convince that maxed-out inner child that you completely understand their fear. You could start with: *Of course you feel that way, because* _____

_____

_____

_____

Looking back on your life, what hidden benefits might you have accrued from having to handle too much too early on your own? What current strengths came from having to take care of things by yourself?

Your fearful child part always has good reasons to feel overwhelmed. Your first job is to validate those reasons. Don't skip that step. It will strengthen you. You can seek solutions later once your scared inner child feels heard.

What is your current philosophy of how to handle stress well? Pretend you found a little fortune cookie message that sums up this mindset. What would it say?

Describe a recent challenging incident that you handled in a way that pleased you. What was it about your response that made you feel good?

Resilience is learned from repeatedly overcoming threats to your safety or well-being. Below, recall two challenging situations from your past and how you got through them:

Looking back on _____, *I feel proud of how I* _____

_____.

Looking back on _____, *I admire how I* _____

_____.

What did you learn about yourself from those experiences?

_____

_____

_____

_____

There are five simple responses for handling any big problem. You can use these empowering actions to increase your resilience:

- **Write** down the problem and figure out what scares you about the situation.

- **Ask** for help as you need it.

- **Break** down the problem into sections, and work stepwise toward the solution.

- **Curb** self-criticism; don't judge yourself.

- **Optimistically** envision how you will feel on the other side of the solved problem.

That last action will calm you right down, and it's the one that EI parents usually don't teach their children because it requires empathy and foresight. EIPs get stuck in their immediate fears too. They can't help their child feel optimistic that they will resolve things and feel good again in the future because they have trouble doing this for themselves.

You can help your scared inner child by using a silly mnemonic—WABCO—for these five problem-solving actions. For practice, fill in each line below:

W _____

A _____

B _____

C _____

O _____

· ·

It's normal to be afraid and uncertain in the face of a new challenge. Just tolerate the discomfort. You don't have to immediately know what to do.

· ·

We all need time to get over the shock of a new problem before we can figure out our next move. *Everybody* goes through a process of uncertainty before they find the first steps. So let's be impertinent and reject that unrealistic pressure to act like you have an instant solution and don't need any help! Declare the following out loud with feeling:

Who says I have to know what to do in every situation?

Where is it written that I have to face all my challenges calmly?

What difference does it make if I get nervous under pressure? I'll still cope.

Give me a short argument explaining why expectations of perfectly calm functioning under stress are totally unrealistic for anyone:

Let's audaciously defend your normal reaction of feeling initially shocked and overwhelmed by unforeseen challenges.

From now on, I won't feel bad about myself when I freak out over a problem. I know that a part of me does that because

I will support my overwhelmed inner child by

A quick check-in: What has it been like for you so far to journal about your very human vulnerability to feeling overwhelmed?

After thinking about all this, tell me why you no longer feel so ashamed of being overwhelmed and scared at times:

_____

_____

_____

_____

How do you see yourself differently now as a result of journaling about this?

_____

_____

_____

_____

How has your resilience improved since you've become aware of how EIPs have impacted you?

_____

_____

_____

_____

Today you get to choose your path for the future. Initial the mindset you choose for yourself going forward:

The path of stagnation: I desperately hide how stunned and disoriented I feel at times. When I have a big problem, I try my best not to show how frightened I am. I keep up a good front and act as though I have it all under control, even if I don't know what to do next. I would feel ashamed to ask others for their help or advice, so I don't.

The path of growth: I aspire to be resilient, not impervious. I accept that events should and do affect me. I try to be authentic with people close to me instead of exhausting myself to keep up a good front. Of course I feel knocked down at times, because I'm human and I lacked emotional support as a child. But I bounce back well once I accept my fears and work with my inner child. I then let my adult self handle it, and I find the right people to consult with, for both emotional support and practical advice.

Contemplating these two paths, how does each one make you feel about your future?

Look ahead and share with me your vision for "resilient you" in the future. Describe how you plan to handle difficult or overwhelming circumstances going forward:

_____

_____

_____

_____

_____

_____

_____

_____

Imagine your higher self applauding how you're working through your emotionally unsupported past as you face challenges in the future. Your higher self sees that you're doing something very different with those overwhelmed feelings now. Listen for a quiet moment, then write what your higher self says to you about your progress in becoming more and more resilient.

_____

_____

_____

_____

_____

PART 9

Be Friendly with Your Mistakes

At this point in your life, you get to decide how to treat yourself. If you treat yourself with pressure and criticism, you will feel bad and have little energy for accomplishing anything. If you treat yourself nicely with respect and guidance, you will have hope and energy to improve your life in a real way.

—*Self-Care for Adult Children of Emotionally Immature Parents* (p. 198)

We all make mistakes and errors of judgment. But when the stakes are high or a situation is unfamiliar, your unsupported inner child might panic and make things worse by attacking your self-worth after making a mistake. It's important to look back and be aware of how childhood influences have affected your attitude toward your inevitable errors.

Accept your mistakes with good humor because self-criticism and feeling bad make it harder to solve the problem at hand.

As you were growing up, how did family members react to your mistakes?

How do *you* treat yourself when you make a mistake? At those times, what does your most self-critical part tell you about yourself?

If you react with self-criticism, how might that affect your willingness to try something new?

_____

_____

_____

Think back to times when you learned most easily. Check the approach that worked best for you:

☐ Someone encouraged me and repeatedly, calmly showed me how to do it.

☐ They looked exasperated, berated me, and impatiently zipped through an explanation.

Now go back and put a star by the approach you want to take with yourself.

Pretend you're doing the voice-over in a movie about an episode in your life when you didn't handle things very well. As that narrator, describe the kind of thoughts and outlook you had that weakened your resilience.

_____

_____

_____

_____

Tell me about someone you remember who handled mistakes particularly well. (This person could be from real life, a movie, a book, the news, or elsewhere.)

Consider your future. Tell me about the kind of attitude you want to have toward your mistakes when life gets difficult.

Let's set an intention right now to develop a self-accepting attitude toward mistakes that will move you forward, not tear you down. Finish the following statement of intention:

From now on, I will try to respond to my mistakes by _____

_____

_____

_____

How might a more optimistic, serene attitude toward mistakes enable you to bounce back more quickly from setbacks or misjudgments?

_____

_____

_____

_____

_____

Is it possible that harsh self-criticism and shame over mistakes may have benefited you in some way? Please elaborate.

_____

_____

_____

At any moment in your life, you get to choose which way you want to go forward. You're the only one who can set your attitude and chart your course. Which of the following paths will you choose? Initial the path that best describes your intention right this minute:

_ _ _ _ _ _ **The path of stagnation:** I make way too many mistakes. I'll never learn if I just blow them off, so I make sure I recognize how serious mistakes are. I plan to beat myself up for "careless" errors that I shouldn't have made in the first place. People will think badly of me if I don't show them how terribly sorry I am for making errors. I intend to be vigilant and try not to make any mistakes in the future. I'll feel awful if I do mess up, so I should criticize myself.

_ _ _ _ _ _ **The path of growth:** It's impossible to be perfect. I'm going to try hard to do the best, most error-free job I can, but I know I'll make mistakes sometimes. If I do, I'll fix them and analyze each mistake so I can do better in the future. If I need to, I'll apologize, but I also know that I'm not a machine and so some errors may slip through.

Which of these paths sounds more reasonable, and which sounds more like the worried child of an EI parent?

_____

_____

_____

_____

_____

Which path do you think your higher self hopes you choose? Why would it be happy about you going in that direction?

If you did change and become more self-forgiving and philosophical about making mistakes, how might that affect your self-image going forward?

PART 10

Find Good People Who Treat You Right

If you grew up with emotionally immature parents, you may feel subconsciously drawn to the familiarity of egocentric and exploitative people.

—*Adult Children of Emotionally Immature Parents* (pp. 177–178)

Your parents and other family members were your original models for close relationships. They taught you how to expect to be treated in a relationship, and that became your script for getting close to other people. Your self-image, your social confidence, and your hopes for happiness grew from these early roots in family living. How you were treated at home undoubtedly created expectations about what you would find in the outside world.

Having emotionally immature parents can have a huge impact on what you expect from future relationships and how comfortable you are in relationships.

EIPs make it seem natural and right for them to be the most important person in any relationship, the one to whom others defer. Most of the time, they feel no obligation to treat you with consideration, respect your boundaries, or listen to your feelings. Their defensiveness and sense of entitlement blind them to their impact on others. With such self-centered people in your early life, inconsiderate behavior may seem familiar or even normal. As an adult, you may still tolerate controlling, self-involved people even when their behavior doesn't merit that second, third, or fourth chance from you. It's all a matter of what you're used to.

EI parents teach their children to tolerate other people's domineering, entitled behavior. They teach this lesson when they treat you with disrespect or coercion, then act insulted if you object or resist. The message from the parent is not just that you're bad for disobeying them—you're bad for even *wanting* to disobey them. For instance, you should feel guilty and selfish for wanting to set boundaries. If you don't see through the extreme unfairness of this, you may fall for the same kind of emotional maneuvers in your adult relationships.

Emotionally absent parenting in childhood can make you willing in adulthood to put up with too much and to be satisfied with too little.

Fortunately, many ACEIPs do seek out kinder, fairer, more emotionally responsive people as they mature. They notice when someone takes their feelings into account and *wants* to know what is going on with them. Nevertheless, past EI patterns can still feel

Did you ever feel like you gave more than you got in your family?

comfortingly familiar, and it's important to spot those old habits so you can free yourself of any remaining self-defeating tendencies in relationships.

In the upcoming journaling section, we'll take a look at how EIPs in your past may have conditioned you to tolerate nonreciprocal behavior in other people or to ignore other warning signs of emotional immaturity.

As a child, did you ever want to run away? Tell me about daydreams you may have had about attaching to other people or homes when you were growing up. What would these other people or places have offered you that you didn't get at home?

For the next two questions, write down what first comes to mind. You can make a note if your parents didn't do these things.

What do you think your mother might tell me if I asked how she prepared you to be treated well in adult relationships?

What might your father say he tried to teach you about what to look out for in relationships?

You probably picked up additional information about close relationships from many sources besides your EI parent. What are some lessons about relationships that you learned from others?

Think about the relationships you had in your immediate family growing up. Using just a few words for each, describe how you felt around each family member.

Consciously or not, a part of you may expect the same responses from other people that you got from your parents.

_____

_____

_____

_____

_____

_____

Now pretend you are watching your childhood from the outside, seeing yourself as a child growing up with these people. Describe what you feel watching this child in their daily family and school-life relationships.

_____

_____

_____

_____

_____

_____

What do you think that child was learning about what to expect from relationships?

Growing up, what did you hope future relationships or friendships would be like?

When you were first dating and socializing as a teen and young adult, if you ever tolerated bad relationships or toxic friendships—just to have some kind of connection—what was it that attracted you to those people?

_____

_____

_____

_____

We can contribute to our own relationship problems by accepting uncaring or inconsiderate behavior. Which of the following self-defeating relationship behaviors have you been most susceptible to in the past? Check all that apply.

☐ You make excuses for other people's self-centered behavior.

☐ You disregard warning signs when someone shows you a red flag about their character.

☐ You mistake the other person's boundary incursions for harmless spontaneity or passionate attraction to you.

☐ You're vulnerable to falling for a person's expression of love or idealization of you, even though they don't know you that well.

☐ You give people repeated chances if they apologize profusely and beg to reunite after treating you badly.

☐ You feel bad when your boundaries upset or anger someone, wondering if you were overly strict or mean.

☐ You interpret control and jealousy as being needed and loved.

☐ You think someone's hurtful criticism and efforts to change you show their interest and investment in your development.

You may have changed over the years, becoming more discerning about problematic relationship patterns. How have you matured since those earlier years?

_____

_____

_____

_____

Which of the following emotionally mature qualities in people do you admire the most and want more of now? Check as many as apply.

- ☐ Generosity, gratitude, thoughtfulness
- ☐ Humor
- ☐ Empathy and consideration for your feelings
- ☐ Respecting your boundaries
- ☐ Ability to stay reasonable under pressure
- ☐ Readiness to have fun and enjoy new experiences
- ☐ Not taking their stress out on other people
- ☐ Receptive listening and "getting" you
- ☐ Willingness to talk about feelings
- ☐ Willingness to negotiate and work things out
- ☐ Readiness to take responsibility for their mistakes
- ☐ Having an organized, responsible attitude about basic duties in life
- ☐ Encouraging your hopes and dreams

With this review in mind, step back now and take a good look at your relationships. Tell me about your level of satisfaction with them.

Who in your life do you feel best with, and why? Who brings out the best in you? Who believed in you before you could believe in yourself?

What are you most proud of about how you are in your present relationships?

Describe the arc of your development from when you were a teenager to where you are now, in terms of your capacity for healthy and fulfilling relationships.

Might there have been any hidden benefits from how you felt growing up in your family relationships? For instance, did it make you more appreciative of kind people, or more wary of exploitative people? Describe a negative relationship you learned a lot from, even if it wasn't a positive experience at the time.

What particular things do you always draw the line at in your current relationships? Where did you learn to do that?

_____

_____

_____

_____

_____

_____

_____

Consider the following empowering statement:

I have the right to trust my instincts to know when I feel loved, respected, and cared for. No one can tell me whom I should love or how much.

If you would like to claim this sense of empowerment, read the statement out loud and then write it out here with intention:

_____

_____

_____

_____

To shake off any lingering feelings of guilt or self-doubt about setting boundaries and being clear about what you don't want, let's show some healthy impertinence toward any relationship that feels emotionally one-sided. Try saying these out loud for practice. (You can decide later if you want to actually say them to anyone.)

- *How can I enjoy being with you when you are critical and try to dictate to me how I should be in our relationship?*
- *How come when I express a preference, you discount it, but when you have a preference, I'm supposed to treat it as sacred?*
- *What's going on here that, between the two of us, you're the one whose feelings always matter most?*

Now try writing a couple of your own impertinent questions!

Make an audacious claim to the kind of relationships you want. Tell me in your own words the kind of people you want to be with now and how you want to feel around them.

A quick check-in: Tell me how it's been so far to think about this topic of relationships.

Do you think that there could've been any benefits to you from having some bad relationships in the past? If so, tell me why.

Here are two possible future paths for you to consider. Initial the one that you now choose:

The path of stagnation: I'm lucky when someone is interested in me at all. I rarely end relationships when they're not right for me because it's preferable to being alone. I believe that everybody deserves the benefit of the doubt and that I shouldn't be too quick to judge someone just because they do things I don't like. I put up with bossy people because it gets worse when I try to set boundaries with them. Who am I to judge? I want to make sure most people like me and I have a good reputation socially.

The path of growth: I notice how people react to my reasonable requests, boundaries, and deeper conversations. I trust my instincts and never feel bad about disliking someone. I'm not obligated to give everyone a fair chance. At the first sign of doubt about someone, I try to figure out what's bothering me about their behavior. If it can't be resolved, I don't have to be in any relationship that makes me feel bad. I want to have fun and feel totally comfortable being myself with someone.

Now let's visualize and imagine yourself going forward as a person who picks relationships consciously and carefully. Try on the following self-image:

I am the kind of person who is always on the lookout for a new friend but quickly notices if they behave in ways that drain me or show incompatibility, self-centeredness, or shallowness. In romance, I am not interested in commitment for its own sake or to keep me from being alone. Instead I give myself time to get to know what kind of person I'm dealing with. I faithfully pay attention to my intuition and notice if there are any red flags or lack of real connection with the person. I know myself and only want to welcome people into my life who treat me kindly and considerately.

Describe how your life would feel if you lived this way.

_____

_____

_____

_____

_____

_____

_____

_____

_____

_____

Now imagine your higher self smiling with delight to see you actively selecting the relationships you want to invest in. Your higher self is so proud of you for treating your time, emotions, and energy as valuable and worthy of protecting from depleting people. It's so glad that you now feel worthy of happiness, respect, and kindness in all your relationships. Take a bow. (I mean it, take a little bow. It's just us here!)

PART II

Find Your Optimal Distance and Watch Those Healing Fantasies

Limit-setting doesn't have to be harsh or controlling; it can just be a positive way of creating space for yourself. Think of it as making room for you, not aggressing against others. Voicing boundaries is just a way of stating your preferences. It's nothing more than being honest about what makes you feel comfortable and safe.

—*Self-Care for Adult Children of Emotionally Immature Parents* (p. 27)

There are plenty of relationships in our lives that we value but which serve us best in small doses. Sometimes we don't want to lose those relationships, but we need to regulate our length and frequency of visits so that we can protect our energy and space enough to enjoy them. Anyone who drains your energy or feels like a struggle to relate to may require you to keep some optimal distance between contacts or visits. You get to decide how much contact is the right amount. This is easy enough to calculate if you think back to how you've felt during visits.

Sometimes you may agree to more contact than you really want because you're holding on to *healing fantasies* (Gibson 2015) of how your loved ones will change someday if you just try hard enough in the relationships. You may hope that showing loyalty and devotion will promote more emotional acceptance and intimacy between you and them. You may hope that if you show them you want to be with them, they will want to be with you.

Your energy level tells you how much time you want to spend with them.

Unfortunately, you can forget to ask yourself this: Is the healing fantasy even something that you still long for? *Do* you still need that person's love and approval in the same way as you did before? And do you sometimes spend more time with them than you want to in hopes that you'll finally have a special moment of real connection?

Tell me about a time when someone in your life made you feel obligated to spend more time with them than was easy, or expected you to do more for them than you really wanted to? What did that feel like?

Have you ever felt duty bound to overlook behaviors that made a person hard to get along with? At the time, why do you think you tolerated that?

_____

_____

_____

_____

_____

_____

For the next two questions, write down what first comes to mind.

If I asked your mother what she taught you about who you're obligated to spend time with and why, what might she say?

_____

_____

_____

If I asked your father about why he thought it was important to spend time with some people you don't like or who are unpleasant toward you, what might he say?

_____

_____

_____

What do you typically do if someone wants to spend more time with you and you are ready to go?

_____

_____

_____

_____

Does family love mean being together for as long as humanly possible?

Imagine how your life would change if you set honest limits on how much time you wanted to spend with someone. If you could control the length of your time together, how might that change how you felt going into the interaction?

_____

_____

_____

_____

_____

What is your healing fantasy? Describe how your EIP would have to change so you two could have more closeness, better understanding, and a deeper connection. (Write this with heart.)

_____

_____

_____

_____

_____

_____

_____

_____

If you were to place a bet, how likely is this change, and why?

_____

_____

_____

_____

Let yourself feel however these odds make you feel. Write it down.

_____

_____

_____

_____

. . . .

_____

_____   *Healing fantasies*
                                               are a child's method
_____   *of holding on to*
                                                  hope. Do you still
_____   *need that hope?*

. . . .   163

Tell me about any experiences you've had with your EIP that show they might be capable of improving your relationship one day.

We'd better pause here in case your answers have put you in touch with the disappointed inner child in you who has not been able to create a closer relationship with that EIP. Listen carefully and write down how that inner child feels about possibly never getting the connection and understanding they have needed for so long.

Tell that emotionally lonely child within you what *you* understand about them. Express your sympathy with their healing fantasy. Explain to them how life might get better if they release the fantasy and depend instead on you and other kind people for empathy and help.

If you're ready to change this dynamic of waiting for your EIP to transform, try copying down the following self-empowering statements with intention, reclaiming your vitality and self-acceptance:

If I find myself wishing someone would change as the answer to my happiness, I give myself a little shake and remember that how I treat myself has the biggest effect on my happiness.

I'm not waiting indefinitely for someone to change. I'm going to pursue what gives me energy so I can live my life with vitality.

Consider the following two paths when it comes to planning the optimal amount of time with people you find difficult to enjoy but hope to be close to one day. Initial the one that you choose going forward:

> **The path of stagnation:** I take my lead for length and frequency of visits from the other person. I don't want to offend anyone by suggesting shorter amounts of time together. They might think I don't like them, and I don't know what I'd say if they confronted me. It's not a big deal because it's just a visit. I can put up with it. Who knows, maybe this visit will be the one to bring us closer. I hope that one day my loved one will soften and treat me better. I look forward to when we finally really talk and feel close to each other.

> **The path of growth:** Before I plan a visit, I always sit down and imagine how I'll feel and how long I want to stay. I tell them in advance how long I can come for, and I politely let them know I can't stay longer. I don't have any illusions that my staying longer will give us a deeper relationship. If they seem to take offense, I tell them how nice they are to want me to stay but tell them that's as long as I can spend this time. I plan for the optimal amount of time it takes to give us a little reunion without making me feel coerced or trapped.

Imagine your higher self applauding as you become more realistic and protect your energy levels in this way. What does your higher self say about your decision to not get too drained by overly long or frequent visits? What does it say about possibly releasing your healing fantasies?

PART 12

Feel Your Value and Vitality in Spite of Their Judgments

Sometimes it is not enough just to have respect for yourself. Sometimes you have to actively protect yourself from people and situations that would drain your energies or hurt your feelings. Looking out for yourself is a primary responsibility, whether it's setting boundaries or making sure that others aren't allowed to limit your life.

—*Self-Care for Adult Children of Emotionally Immature Parents* (p. 23)

You can't criticize a child into self-esteem. EI parents really have no idea how to nurture confidence and vitality in their children, or how to help a child develop a solid sense of their value as a human being. EI parents lack that holistic sense of their child as a separate, real individual on a developmental path of their own. Instead of grasping the child's unique nature and helping them feel good about who they naturally are, EI parents assess their children superficially, focusing on external behaviors and characteristics that they judge with criticism or approval.

The EI parent thinks they are doing their duty by correcting and socializing their child, but many times they are actually making their child feel unsafe about being authentic. EI parents forget that what they disapprove of is part of a sensitive young human being who is trying to find themselves and feel confident about their place in life.

EIPs aren't necessarily trying to be mean; it's just that their rigidity drives them to correct anything they see as undesirable.

When your parent gives you the feeling that, in order to please them, you have to continually monitor your behavior and presentation, they zap your inborn self-confidence and vitality. When you feel like you have to be something more than just yourself, you become an object of your own scrutiny, sizing yourself up and worrying about your worthiness. Your natural energy and liveliness drain away under this spotlight of self-evaluation.

How can you feel enthusiastic and vibrant when you're not even sure you have a right to be here just as you are?

Once you take a parent's critical and judgmental tendencies to heart, you become divided within yourself. Part of your mind becomes dedicated to self-evaluation. One part of you wants to express itself, while another part is rendering a verdict on whether that's acceptable. This self-scrutiny is stifling to creativity, spontaneity, and self-expression. Your mind begins to stutter-step a little, hesitating for that split second to make sure you're not going to be corrected. Humor, joy, and playfulness wilt in this atmosphere of self-doubt; it's no longer easy to be yourself. If you can't be yourself, you can't be joyful—and if you shut off joy, you shut off vitality and all the things that go with it, like fascination, motivation, eagerness, and the urge to create things.

Vitality depends on the free flow of joy, optimism, and spontaneity in your daily life. When you are feeling this inner energy, you feel like it's okay to be yourself, to be imaginative, to like the things you like, and to enjoy the ideas that pop into your head. One part of your brain is not set against another, and there's no shame or self-judgment going on. You are just you freely being you.

As a child, you may have been willing to suppress some of your energy so you wouldn't offend or annoy anyone.

In this section, you're going to think about how you may have sacrificed your vitality and sense of worth through a misguided effort to gain approval from EIPs. We're going to take a look at how their judgments may have diminished your natural enthusiasm and confidence.

Pleasing others is never worth an alienation from your true self.

Let's think about how an EI parent's readiness to analyze and criticize may have impacted your feelings about your own inherent worth. Many children think that their attempts at self-improvement and conformity will one day earn their parents' love and respect. But the security you sought from parental approval is already yours for the taking as soon as you start seeing both them and yourself with realism and clarity.

Describe which of your childhood attitudes or behaviors were most likely to bring criticism or judgment from your EI parent.

As an adult now, what kinds of situations are most capable of making you become intensely self-critical?

For the next two questions, write down what first comes to mind. If your parents didn't make efforts in this direction, you can say that too.

If I asked your mother how she tried to make you feel good about yourself and encourage your vitality, what might she say?

If I asked your father how he tried to nourish your self-esteem and keep your spirits up, what might he say?

Which people in your childhood environment gave you the most *positive* feeling about your value as a person? How did they do that?

Which people in your childhood had the most *dampening* effect on your vitality—your playfulness, expressiveness, or enthusiasm? How did they do that?

Think back to when you were a child, to a memory of yourself when you were full of energy and interest. Describe the activity you were involved in, and pretend you are watching yourself totally immersed in it. What was it about that moment that brought out this vitality in you?

Now think back to times when you truly felt valued as an individual, like you were somebody who mattered. Who made you feel good about yourself and free to be lively and spontaneous? What about this person made you feel that way?

Was there a turning point in your life when you became more self-critical, inhibiting, or judgmental toward yourself? How old were you, and why do you think it happened then?

Under what circumstances do you now become self-conscious and judge yourself? What kinds of things do you say to yourself at those times?

What would you like your critics—the ones who made you self-conscious and fearful of annoying them—to know about their impact on you? If they did want to know how they had negatively impacted you, what would you tell them? (This entry is for your eyes only.)

What if they were never going to make you feel good about yourself or encourage your sense of value and vitality? Could you do that for yourself, even if nobody else changed? How do you feel about making this change for yourself?

_____

_____

_____

_____

_____

_____

Do you think any good has come out of feeling criticized? Are there benefits you derived from inhibiting your spontaneity or worrying about what people would think?

_____

_____

_____

_____

_____

_____

Let's try out some more impertinent thoughts to rebuff judgment and reclaim your natural liveliness, regardless of EIPs' opinions. Finish these sentences with the first thoughts that pop into your mind:

Even though you've made me second-guess myself, I'm not falling for it anymore. From here on, I'm going to _____

_____.

What gave you the right to make me feel so _____

_____?

Too bad if you think I should be different. From now on, I'm going to _____

_____.

A quick check-in: What has this been like for you so far to journal about judgmental people and their effect on your spontaneity and sense of self-value?

_____

_____

_____

_____

_____

Which of the following two paths most appeals to you? Initial the one that you choose going forward:

_ _ _ _ _ _   **The path of stagnation:** Other people must have reasons for being judgmental toward me. I need to consider their criticisms carefully and monitor myself to be the best version of myself that others will like. Self-inhibition is good because it keeps me from coming on too strong and alienating people. I don't want to get too full of myself or get on others' nerves, so I keep myself a little subdued. What I want most is to be liked and accepted.

_ _ _ _ _ _   **The path of growth:** When anyone makes me feel emotionally lonely or unsure of my worth, I keep a healthy distance. I'm realistic about how much change I can expect from anybody. I look for people who make me feel good and share meaningful interests. I learn from my mistakes, but don't beat myself up. I like my spontaneous real self and view myself compassionately. When I am not sure how to proceed, I trust my intuition and feel which alternatives lift (or lower) my energy. My vitality and energy levels are crucial to protect for my emotional health.

How do you think your life would be different if you kept your distance from critical people, gave up hope for changing them, and looked for relationships that increase your energy rather than your self-doubt?

_____

_____

_____

_____

Imagine that your higher self has been happily watching your development into a more vital, self-assured, self-possessed person with good boundaries, holding the line against anyone who might lower your spirits. Imagine that it is excited about your progress and is giving you a standing ovation for rejecting unneeded criticism and freeing yourself from judgmental relationships. Give yourself a moment to soak this in and feel how far you've come. What changes in you are you especially proud of?

Finally, what have you realized the most over the course of this journal? Which aspects of your needs do you now take more seriously, and what did you learn most about how EIPs have impacted your life?

_____

_____

_____

_____

_____

_____

_____

_____

_____

_____

_____

_____

_____

_____

Afterword

I have decided I don't have to know where the soul comes from. I just have to acknowledge that there is something inside that energizes and guides us.

—*Self-Care for Adult Children of Emotionally Immature Parents* (p. 21)

Your journey through this journal has been an encounter with yourself—past, present, and future. You've realized at a deep level how EIPs have impacted your experience of yourself and your life. I hope you discovered some new things about yourself, and I hope these insights pay off in your future.

Some questions may have been hard to answer, or the answers might have surprised you. But I wanted to provide you with new perspectives, a little different from your everyday thoughts. Hopefully, you've come to understand how your past may have affected your ability to actualize your most vibrant individuality. Understanding yourself in the past as a child can be just as important and productive as imagining what you want to become as an adult, because understanding your past changes how you narrate your future.

By filling out this journal, you've created a record of your life under the influence of EIPs. You can go back through these pages and trace your progress from trying to please others to reuniting with the emotionally alive, connected, and free-thinking individual that you've been all along. I hope you find it easier now to brush off the cobwebs of outdated assumptions and coercive loyalties. By rereading what you've written, you can even function like a new parent to yourself and nurture all parts of yourself into a new maturity.

My hope is that by increasing your self-knowledge in this journal (and occasionally having some fun with audacious impertinence), you've started to question why you should give so much credence to people who can't see beyond their own opinions, who can neither support you nor relate to who you really are. They may have had a big impact on your life, but I think you can now see how to escape their influence in order to live your own life. You can still love them, you can honor them, but don't let them have your future. They have been given their lifetime; yours is up to you.

I also hope that you've taken some long, hard looks down those two alternate paths to the future—stagnation and growth—so that what you want for the rest of your life is now clearer as a result. All it takes to change is the awareness of what has happened to you and consciousness of where you want to go next.

I like to think that we have a higher-self part that watches over our development. It's the part that knows what we're capable of and wants us to find our true self. Think of it as the soul of your emerging maturity. I'm sure it gets excited every time you win back another little piece of yourself. You're never alone on this journey. **Your higher self and I are over here smiling at your progress; we can't wait to see what you're going to do next.**

Acknowledgments

I am grateful beyond words to my husband, Skip Gibson; my sister, Mary Babcock; my son, Carter, and his husband, Nick; and my friends and family who have been such wonderful supporters during the process of creating this journal.

Thank you to Tesilya Hanauer at New Harbinger Publications for bringing this journal to the world, and to Madison Davis and Karen Schader for making it the best it could be.

My sincerest appreciation to all the readers, podcasters, and clients who have spread the word about the effects of emotional immaturity on people's lives.

References

Anderson, C. *The Stages of Life*. New York: Atlantic Monthly Press.

Clance, P. R. 2017. *The Imposter Phenomenon*. Atlanta, GA: Peachtree Publishers.

Gibson, L. C. 2015. *Adult Children of Emotionally Immature Parents*. Oakland, CA: New Harbinger Publications.

———. 2019. *Recovering from Emotionally Immature Parents*. Oakland, CA: New Harbinger Publications.

———. 2021. *Self-Care for Adult Children of Emotionally Immature Parents*. Oakland, CA: New Harbinger Publications.

———. 2023. *Disentangling from Emotionally Immature People*. Oakland, CA: New Harbinger Publications.

Jung, C. 1997. *Jung on Active Imagination*. Edited by J. Chodorow. Princeton, NJ: Princeton University Press.

Schwartz, R. 1995. *Internal Family Systems Therapy*. New York: Guilford Press.

Shaw, D. 2014. *Traumatic Narcissism*. New York: Routledge.

Whitfield, C. L. 1987. *Healing the Child Within*. Deerfield Beach, FL: Health Communications.

Winnicott, D. W. 1989. *Psychoanalytic Explorations*. Edited by C. Winnicott, R. Shepherd, and M. Davis. New York: Routledge Books.

Also by Lindsay C. Gibson

ISBN 978-1626251700 / US $18.95

ISBN 978-1684032525 / US $16.95

ISBN 978-1684039821 / US $17.95

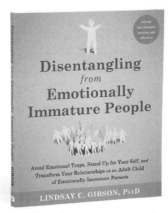

ISBN 978-1648481512 / US $21.95

 new**harbinger**publications

1-800-748-6273 / newharbinger.com

LINDSAY C. GIBSON, PsyD, is a clinical psychologist and psychotherapist with more than thirty years' experience working in both public service and private practice. Her books—including the #1 Amazon best seller, *Adult Children of Emotionally Immature Parents*—have sold more than a million copies, and have been translated into thirty-four languages. In the past, Gibson has served as an adjunct assistant professor, teaching doctoral clinical psychology students clinical theory and psychotherapy techniques. She specializes in therapy and coaching with adults to attain new levels of personal growth, emotional intimacy with others, and confidence in dealing with emotionally immature family members. Her website is available at www.lindsay gibsonpsyd.com. Gibson lives and works in Virginia Beach, VA.

Did you know there are **free tools** you can download for this book?

Free tools are things like **worksheets**, **guided meditation exercises**, and **more** that will help you get the most out of your book.

You can download free tools for this book— whether you bought or borrowed it, in any format, from any source—from the New Harbinger website. All you need is a NewHarbinger.com account. Just use the URL provided in this book to view the free tools that are available for it. Then, click on the "download" button for the free tool you want, and follow the prompts that appear to log in to your NewHarbinger.com account and download the material.

You can also save the free tools for this book to your **Free Tools Library** so you can access them again anytime, just by logging in to your account! Just look for this button on the book's free tools page.

+ Save this to my free tools library

If you need help accessing or downloading free tools, visit **newharbinger.com/faq** or contact us at **customerservice@newharbinger.com**.